The Morning After Burns Night

The Morning After Burns Night

Poems by

Joyce Wilson

Cover design by Shay Culligan
Cover image *Red Sky Morning at Minot Beach* (2022)
by Joyce Wilson
Internal images from Unsplash; respectively, by
MD Shariful Islam (dedication), DA Vector (prelude),
godsfavoriteart (I), DA Vector (II), Anna Magenta (III)
Author photo *Joyce at L'Horloge Fleurie de Genève
dans le Jardin Anglais* (2024) by John Goldie

ISBN: 979-8-90146-986-6
Library of Congress Control Number: 2026939011

Kelsay Books
502 South 1040 East, A-119
American Fork, Utah 84003
Kelsaybooks.com

for the unrequited

Acknowledgments

Poems appeared in the following literary journals, some in slightly different form, under different titles:

Constellations: "Where No One Else Has Gone" (as "Driving Through Southern Lebanon")
Free Inquiry: "Iambic Translation," "On Lichens"
The Hudson Review: "To a Deer Tick"
Ibbetson Street Magazine: "Maps," "The Wild Turkeys Return," "Ben Franklin Nominates the Wild Turkey as the National Bird," "Bad Dream"
Light Magazine: "On Leaves," "Entropy of Spring"
Lighten Up Online: "A Whale Entangled"
The Lyric: "Two Dogs," "A Recipe for Gratitude" (as "Making Jelly from Grapes")
The Lyric's Roberts Memorial Prize (1st place, 2022): "Two Dogs"
Mezzo Cammin: "The Rockettes Appear on the Tonight Show," "Jumping Spider of My Mind," "Lamartine in Lebanon," "Afternoon Prayers at the Maronite Chapel in Beirut"
Muddy River Poetry Review: "Eurydice"
The Orchards Poetry Journal: "Domestic Shorthair"
Poetry by the Sea Poetry Conference's Kim Bridgford Contest (Honorable Mention, 2020): "The Remnant of His Life" (as "The Ritual Bath")
The Poetry Porch: "The Women in the Church," "Unsigned Memorials to Mary"
Slant: "Negotiations" (as "The Marriage Robe")
The Sonnet Scroll of The Poetry Porch: "The Remnant of His Life"
Think: "Beirut Garden," "The Sacred Cedars"

Contents

II. The Remnant of His Life: A Sonnet Crown

III. Driving Through Southern Lebanon

Prelude

The Morning After Burns Night

1. *The morning after*

Blue sky, all the way to Portugal,
and planes off to New York, engines in tune.
Atlantic surf exploding on our sea wall
as if it would destroy it by high noon.

The news announced a Middle East cease fire
that was broken and again renewed,
and statesmen vowed no refugees for hire
while others watched as tempers flared and stewed.

We found the eggs our hens had hid away,
despite the deep freeze overnight, each one
a sign of spring, we often liked to say,
of longer days and shorter nights to come.

2. *The night before*

It all began when Martin took a breath
and brought alive an image from the past,
and summoned all his strength, and exiled death's
complacency, with his best bagpipe blast,

while Alice, reaching out to our old dog,
who hates to be picked up, hugged Orpheo,
who praised the wine and spiked eggnog
by summoning melodies from the piano,

and Oscar kept a syncopated beat
with a screwdriver, improvised baton,
as Marie sang lyrics to the songs we thought
she knew, yet made up as she went along.

We introduced our poems and our verses
about our friends, the ones both here and gone,
and pairs of things, like lovers' vows and curses,
without regret, from now, and from now on.

I.
Singles and Pairs

A Haven for the White Deer

We talk at length but never seem to know
What's going on, how wars will start and wars
Will end, until munitions left in stores
Of bunkers, now obscured in weeds and snow,

Are all that's left of this old army base,
And why it has become a haven deer
Would seek, to raise their young from year to year,
Is something of a special unsolved case.

Most deer we know will forage in the night
And keep their profiles dark, as shadows go,
To disappear with winter's ebb and flow.
But these arrive in glowing forms of white.

One day at dusk, we met up with a doe
Who trained her eyes on us, as if aware
That we, behind the headlight's blinding glare,
Were suffering the worst of winter's woe.

And then as if ignited from afar,
Her heart began to glow like candlelight,
Emitting rays of wonder, shining bright,
That warmed us like the embers of a star.

Wild Turkeys Return

High-shouldered and bony, they venture near.
Their awkwardness apparent in their walk,
They stand too big to hide, too shy to talk
Yet chirrup to dissuade us of our fear.

As they survey this wind-swept acre's lawn,
We ask ourselves what messages they bear
And what our duties are, if we should dare
To shoo them back to woods, their rightful home,

If we should seek the lessons they might teach,
That once exiled they now return in force
To take their place and reclaim what was theirs.
We watch them slowly draggle out of reach.

We want to love them, on whom much depends—
Our gratitude for nature, sunlight's jewel,
The notion that their coming means renewal—
A second chance for us, their awkward friends.

Two Dogs

I drop a leash. The Other picks it up
To help me out, especially to tup

The One, who catches every ball that's tossed,
Then cries, a baby when the ball is lost.

The Other watches, waiting for his chance.
With ball in mouth, he lengthens his advance.

***

One walks on water as he'd cross a field,
Then sinks in tidal wavelets, forced to yield.

The Other sees the ocean as a threat,
Is horrified that One has gotten wet.

Whenever One will try to slip away,
The Other's bark is heard across the bay.

***

And even now, although the One has died,
The Other barks to bring him to his side.

He listens for his step across the green,
Will know him when he comes. Months intervene.

The Other starts to stretch his limbs and run.
Then he is not thc Other; he's the One.

Domestic Shorthair

In the middle of the night, he comes to me
And throws his back against my side and purrs.
I know his purring rolls not just for me
But for his appetite. His hunger whirs.

When I get up to make the daily dish
That I provide for him, his kibble stew,
I know it's not the sparrow he might wish
To have. Still, no one loves him as I do,

Nor cares as much, and so I squeeze him tight.
And then I sense my fervor has profaned
His trust. He grasps my arm as if to bite
The hand that feeds—at first with claws restrained—

Then draws his hind legs up, as in the wild
He'd rake his prey to shreds, his frenzy riled.

Maps

Maps inspire the traveler
Where a line of chalk
Drawn across a mountain range
Never thought to walk.

Maps across the desk veneer
Cannot feel the points
Where the worried mountaineer
Wants to test his joints.

Maps are to the calendar
What the future tense
To the gipsy with an orb
Hopes will pay her rents.

Maps are to the mountaintop
As a misty gown
O’er the body underneath
Leads the climbers on.

Mythology of Mountains

Mountains hide a goddess
Which the climber stirred
When the naked girl he saw
Flew away a bird.

But that is what the myth opined,
And you might think I'm crude
If I insist he went to find
Not her, but solitude.

To a Deer Tick

Invasive and far flung,
You made yourself at home,
Then loosed your dreadful tongue
To spread your awful foam,

And raised your cup to toast
Your intimate, the deer,
A once distinguished host,
Now feverish, I fear.

To make our day complete,
You left your precious stash:
Your gift a spirochete,
Your calling card a rash.

How rude of you to die
Before we'd said good-bye.

Entropy of Spring

The sack of cracked corn is bulging and round
but slims as soon as I lift it
and kernels pour out in a liquified stream
through the hole where a field mouse has bit it.

After arranging our peony blooms
in colors that cluster and chatter,
I lift up the elegant porcelain vase
to watch petals tumble and scatter.

Even worse is my nose, a passage for stuff
like lava, contained by a faucet
until it escapes and reaches my lip
where only a tissue can sop it.

Then raising the lid of the washing machine
to take out my favorite shirt,
I find the remains of the tissue in shreds
that should have dissolved with the dirt.

Eurydice

After the reading, I followed you
from the darkened auditorium
into the light. I wanted to say
how much I admired your work just then,

yet if I said too much too soon,
I might have persuaded you to turn,
and if you turned to look at me,
to assess your influence on me,

we would have been lost to each other,
and chastened by my vanity,
I might have doubted what I'd said.

When alone, I'd read your book.
The music would release itself
in shadows that I'd make my own.

Bad Dream

The smaller dog, his jaws around the skull
of his messmate, attaches to the hull

of the ungainly ship they make. They race
as if there's no escape from the embrace

that unifies, caught in a darkened sea
much like the pair I never thought I'd see

until the year I watched a colleague strain
to siphon off another's fertile brain.

They floated off into a bleak surround
like Dante's fastened pair, forever bound.

Ben Franklin Nominates the Wild Turkey as the National Bird

The homely favorite of the sly old man,
He seems nearsighted in the way he walks
As he makes his way across the span,
Uncertain when he lifts his head and gawks.

We meet him daily, out and on the prowl,
In search of something that he left behind,
An attitude befitting of a fowl
Who likes to argue, gesture, and be kind.

Now here he comes, with gleaming chest unfluffed
And tail outspread in circular display,
Who holds his wings curled low and fisticuffed,
Advancing as Kabuki dancers may,

A large, top-heavy, self-respecting bird,
Who gabbles by design, true to his word.

Jumping Spider of My Mind

Was it because I turned the faucet handle
That she emerged from hiding, pincers taut
In antic dance, part scurry and part scramble
To chase the glimmer of elusive thought?

She skimmed the counter as if she'd measure
Each plane and fault with palm and underside
Of her being, then made a quick seizure
Of its surface, to finish with a slide

Into the sink, across the dip and down.
Wouldn't she have known where the gleaming edge is
By now? She's out, over the rim and gone,
Casting a line to unseen distant bridges.

How often does she wait behind the spigot
Winding silk to snare her catch, confined
By nervous appetite, or fear of its
Release, this jumping spider of my mind?

The Giant Blue Lactuca

Lactuca biennis

1

An annual among perennials
Like corn gone wild, or six-foot dandelion,

Whose center stem bears heavy yellow sap,
Not sweet water of lettuce, after whom

It has been named, but—imagine it, a cactus,
The succulent that it has just become!—

With horizontal sproutlets reaching out
Above the tiger lilies in their beds,

And topknot crown, much like a spray, or bunch
Of tiny asters, bursting into foam.

2

It lends itself to tales of lost heroes
Who come disguised, unknown, and frighten us,

Whose features seem so strange that they repel
Even as they beckon us to follow

On blue serrated leaves grown hard like rungs
That Jacob's followers could clamber up

As it is sung in Jacob's ladder song,
On which a boy could make a sweet ascent

Through clouds where hungry ogres hoard their gold.
Then we remember what the Bible says

About Goliath, big feet overnight,
Like other giants in our lives who make

A noise and knock till we awake to see
Someone we fear; yet how, with ties to Orpah,

Ruth's sister, he's David's distant cousin,
And scrawny David fells him with a sling!

3

This plant stands tall till frost, then drops its seeds
And falls, stretching out to sleep, to dream

Its winter dreams about the garden plot
That welcomed it, a stranger in our midst,

Stealth invader, prompting us to ask,
Have you come to love or to destroy?

Negotiations

Cairo, 1989

The gift shop near the Pyramids was full
    of djellabas, all types and shapes.
The young Egyptian boy suggested rose
    on black, with blue and gold, but I
knew it would be too small. I touched the folds
    of fine batiste, the softest weave
embroidered with ivory, white on white,
    "This one!" I said and held it up.

"Too big for you. It's for a man," he said.
    A marriage robe made strictly for the groom.
His father suddenly appeared and asked,
    "Perhaps a gift for Christmas night?"
"We call it Eve," I nearly said, as if
    correcting him, but froze before I risked
the naming of that woman most maligned.
    He tucked my purchase in a flimsy bag,

blessed me, turned, then quickly disappeared
    before I could choose something I'd regret.
"Please keep the change," I said, amazed at all
    the civil lies we kept behind our smiles,
an insult ransomed, precious goods for cash,
    withholding that the ceremonial
to him was something casual to me,
    that I would wear at home; and yet, who would

deny me the moment I might find this gown
    of white batiste and fine embroidery
hidden in my closet, where I would put
    it on, the perfect thing to wear, as I
walked through the desert to the Promised Land?

Villanelle as a Film Review

After seeing A Most Wanted Man

Phillip Seymour Hoffman filled the part
Of Bachmann's geezer spy who led the sting
And loved each time he lifted up his eyes.

While Guinness probed the role, was wry and smart
And sealed the way to master Smiley's zing,
Phillip Seymour Hoffman filled the part.

Actor Bannen caught Prideau, his start
Abroad, who bore a wound to serve the King.
He loved each time he lifted up his eyes.

A different time demands a different art.
To gamble that his wheezing lungs would swing,
Phillip Seymour Hoffman filled the part.

Part man, part horse, he loaded up the cart.
Too bad he never heard the fat girl sing
But loved each time he lifted up his eyes.

He gave his life but meant to give his heart.
We thought he held the world upon a string.
Phillip Seymour Hoffman filled the part
And loved each time he lifted up his eyes.

Villanelle for a Portly Rose

Once I believed I was your perfect mate,
The slender thorn to you, the portly rose.
But now you say you've finally lost some weight.

I'm startled, deeply, by this twist of fate.
You're shopping for a sleeker set of clothes.
Once I believed I was your perfect mate

And we the perfect pair, out on a date.
I never thought we'd ever come to blows
About the fact that you had lost some weight.

You leave your dinner untouched on your plate
And tell the waitress, "Thank you. None of those!"
When once you loved to eat, the perfect mate.

You rumble like an engine free of freight
Then turn to strike a Giacometti pose
If someone says, "I see you've lost some weight!"

I wonder if this change has come too late.
How quickly will your friends become your foes?
What is my future as your perfect mate
Now that, it's clear, you've finally lost some weight?

Limericks:
The Rockettes Appear on The Tonight Show

In the past The Rockettes made us laugh.
The sexism seemed like a gaffe,
The look and the sound
Obscurity bound
Beside the endangered giraffe.

It's been years, now we're used to the form.
The costumes are part of the norm.
The legs that advance
A synchronized dance
Have taken our senses by storm.

When the tap dancers kick up a breeze
As holidays put on the squeeze,
It isn't a sin—
We like all the skin!
('Though I couldn't do it. Bad knees.)

You remember the Walgreen's cashier,
The tall skinny girl without fear?
She's living her dream
To work for the team
That magnifies holiday cheer.

Limericks:
A Whale Entangled

O how it makes my heart pale
To think of the fate of a whale
With four thousand pounds
Of gear that surrounds
Its mouth and its torso and tail.

To think of the effort it took
With cutter and hacksaw and hook
And oversized pliers
To cut through the wires
That fisherman dragged and forsook.

Three days, and they cut the whale free
And ushered it out to the sea
To swim with the cod
And frolic with God
Who watches o'er fishes and me.

On Leaves

The officer on duty was amused
By neighbors who complained they were abused
When, on one side, a resident was drawn
To blowing leaves into another’s lawn,

While, standing where the boundary divides,
He found more leaves had fallen on both sides.
It seemed the leaves were only being fair
By falling generally, and everywhere.

A Recipe for Gratitude

The grapes announce the end of their season
when they infuse the air with perfume from
their ripening fruit, a pleasure that engulfs
me when I walk out past the sunlit vines.
In gratitude I want to do my part
to be included in the harvesting,
the transformations that will come about
with changes in the sunlight and the weather.
The jelly that I make will keep the present
sweet, in bunches of the purple grapes,
enough to fill the boiling pot and show
that I can make something out of nothing,
change fruit to juice with sugar over heat
till it expands in bubbly tides of pink
then settles down at last to do its work
and thicken into jiggly gel magic.
And even though whatever I create
will be consumed one morning at breakfast,
to join the temporary of this world,
I will not grieve the loss of my reward,
for I'll be heading somewhere else, to trim
the branches, rake the leaves, all for these vines,
that they might live another hundred years
for my neighbors, the neighborhood, the land.
And I'll be thinking of the seasons when
my friend returns an empty jelly jar
as I hang up the tools where they belong
and ask about her plans for Thanksgiving.

Prose Poem:
Habitat Ramblers

Our infrared camera shows us how our garden, an open cultivated space without enclosure, is a network of avenues and meeting places for animals and birds we don't often see. We set off the rectangular space through our labors weeding and digging, but not by a fence. We clear paths, where weeds crowd in and up between the rows, out of duty and practicality, to take care of our crop, and on these paths the night creatures come. What is to stop them? They seem to monitor the progress of our efforts, the lengthening corn cobs and reddening tomatoes, widening chard and lettuce, waiting until each is ripe for a sample taste. Sometimes we find the stems leaning with a crook in the middle or broken off and dragged a foot or two. Sometimes tomatoes are lying on the ground, a hole gaping, the result of a big bite, although only partially devoured. The deer take all summer to discover the parsley. A beautiful clump of glossy leaves, the combination of six plants that has grown to the size of a beach ball, is reduced to stubble overnight. Only deer would eat the entirety like that. But we should not malign them with curses—not even under our breath—because this is their land. We welcome their intrusion as a firm reminder that they are aware of what we do. And so they help themselves.

Prose Poem:
On Lichens

I found a maple branch on the ground after a windstorm, bearing growths of lichens varying in appearance: one coating the length of the branch like a skin treatment, another like moss with gray berries, and a third like lettuce unfurling its leaves. Apparently, they live off the air and their growth is a sign of good air quality. Looking up at the crown of our maple tree, I can see lichen clusters at the ends of many branches like lacey ornaments, facing the east wind that comes over the hill from the ocean. Botanists say that lichens are some of the oldest living things, and that they like to establish themselves on surfaces that are still and inert. They do not harm the trees and vegetation that they cling to, and yet they are a sign of slow growth and even a reduced vitality. We must admit that our maple tree is getting on in years. When we take walks this winter, we plan to keep looking around for lichens in our favorite wandering places. Where lichens appear, we will stop, look, and take a measure of changes and renewal around us.

II.
The Remnant of His Life:
A Sonnet Crown

The Date

The calendar was hanging by the stair.
The date had loomed like other dates to mark
The progress of their lives, with time to spare
And space for joy, before he'd disembark.

She liked to be of use, and in control,
Was happiest when busying about
The centers and peripheries her role
Assumed, although she now had cause for doubt.

For now that they determined that his end
Was near, she would not go where he would go.
The days began transformed, as if the bend
In time had loosed what once had held them so.

Each moment rose and carried them as they
Reached up and threw the calendar away.

The Place

They reached and threw the calendar away.
He chose the place, an unobstructed view
Of azure sky and treetops on the bay.
He lay down on the bed as if on cue,

Regarding them, bemused through Ativan.
And just as she had seen he was resigned,
She watched him fade as in a caravan
Drawn over mountain paths he'd left behind.

The clock was not rewound. The chimes had rung.
To ease the dryness inside mouth and cheek,
The hospice nurses swabbed his mottled tongue.
The morphine helped him rally through the week.

Would panic seize her when he died? She knew
That she might cry, how much she needed to.

The Undressing

She feared she'd cry, how much she needed to,
As rushing breath-bleats ceased. She brought the cloth,
The shallow bowl, and stirred the magic brew
To salve the end, the stiffening of death.

He was not warm. He would not need these socks,
This button-down that never seemed to fit,
Much like the job that sealed him in a box
No matter how he'd worked to open it.

He would be free of that old struggle now.
Yet how she longed to play the major role
Of liberator standing at the prow,
Where she might claim possession of his soul.

Anxiety, that they'd be forced apart,
Compelled the vision for a greater art.

The Bath

In need of vision for a greater art,
She soaked the cloth and pressed the herbal dregs.
Beginning with his face and neck, she'd start
With head and torso, then his arms and legs.

Was he her lover now? How odd to think
About his hair and nails, that they would grow
Despite the skin's propensity to shrink.
She smelled a lurking fear, decay's shadow.

She stood and took a last good look at him.
His dull repose was more than she could bear.
Part man, part thing, as if behind a scrim,
His stillness struck a chord; not here, not there.

She'd been his guard, through happiness and strife;
She savored this, the remnant of his life.

The Stranger

She savored this, the remnant of his life,
Assessed his ravaged limbs, the twisted band
That failed him once, then twice, as if a knife
Had severed orders from their lone command.

How he had needed her, and she had been
So good, with the appointments, the respect,
The hopes she raised, to see them fall again,
While signs of the disease remained intact.

How valiantly he'd borne each prize, to lose
The lust for life that took him to Nepal,
The classic melodies he'd brought to blues,
The analytic phrase beyond recall.

The humor that sustained the invalid
Had flown. It seemed he was an alien.

The Robe and the Rings

Now that it seemed he was an alien,
That he was gone, eternally his own,
His body would return to dust. And then
She'd do no more than love what she had known.

She robed him in his favorite flannel shirt,
Took off her wedding rings, and pressed them both
In his breast pocket. I should sing, she thought,
And took a breath, and then she found the note,

The tone that brought them into harmony.
She held it as she joined the outer room
Where she would be with friends and family
Who waited, eager to make time resume.

Thus he had gone with all the dignity
That he had sought, a quiet victory.

The Crown

Thus he had gone in quiet victory.
His fear of dying without dignity
Had flown. Although he seemed an alien
Without the hope that blessed the invalid,

She'd cleansed his body, remnant of his life,
Had been his guard through happiness and strife.
Compelled through vision for a greater art,
She'd lost her fear that they'd be forced apart,

That she might cry, how much she needed to.
And no one panicked when he died. She knew
That time would rise and carry them as they
Reached up and threw the calendar away,

The one that mapped their passion and despair,
That she'd retrieve and hang above the stair.

III.
Driving Through Southern Lebanon

Where No One Else Has Gone

It is a delight to go where none has gone before.
—Virgil

Decades after the Civil War, we drive
Through this remote and isolated town

And marvel how the setting holds a modest
Beauty no one else has seen or known,

Far from the urban crowds and offices,
Ill-suited to the theater of war.

Yet we are wrong. The armies have been here,
And what we like they also liked as much:

The rounded cliffs that hug the roadside nook,
The Christian church, the terraced olive groves,

The slope where they could plan the next attack,
Then dig a ditch and leave a roadside bomb.

The sand that lifts and spreads across the road
Obscures the traces of the ones now gone.

Iambic Translation

This evening, we examine The Koran
Where the Prayer of the Cataclysm explains
How in the aftermath of the great deluge
"Each soul shall know what it has done and what
It has failed to do." The few familiar words
Weigh heavy in my throat till it constricts.

They show, like stones across an endless gulf,
How we might boast of something in common—
A patriarchal God full of wrath,
The rising of a flood, the final day,
A love of music and poetic lines—
If only words did not wreak with silence!

Meanwhile my friends insist the problem lies
With Darwood's translation, saying it's too English.

Lamartine in Lebanon

By traveling across the Middle East,
He sought to find the brilliant colors of
That great poem he had in mind, his life,

Beset by doubts and old perplexities
He'd born since childhood, he hoped, abroad,
That they'd be solved, untangled, and explained,

The way our dreams at night illuminate
Those oddities and thoughts we hold by day.
And his enthusiasm found the key

In these great monuments of nature, cedars
Named in passages Ezekiel
Described and set forever in our minds,

Whose fronds of evergreen King Solomon
Had picked to decorate the temple walls
Where first he celebrated the One God.

These trees, as witnessed by the Arab scribes,
Were sensitive to seasons and the snow,
Reaching up at change of temperature

And wide to offer shade for wanderers
Of many creeds from human races past
Who spoke the name of God in different tongues.

What they might tell, if only they could speak!
Of conversations held from age to age
And whispered in the shelter of their shade.

While bearing close the loss of a daughter, he
Got down beneath one great majestic grove
And knelt in place to weep on hallowed ground.

He pressed himself against the history
Unspoken in the thing, its darkest core,
Where silence deepened in a hidden spring.

The Sacred Cedars

"The Cedars know the history of the earth
Better than history itself." So wrote
De Lamartine in Eighteen Thirty-two.

What makes them prosper where the others fail?
Diminishing in number, they endure
Even as their groves bear yellow leaves.

The villagers who come to pray beneath
The oldest canopies of their great boughs
Have long believed in their intelligence,

Which knows the thing better than the story of
The thing, the dark core within the body of
The form, embraced between the green branches.

Afternoon Prayers at the Maronite Chapel in Beirut

We'd been to the Archdiocese before
To ask about the lost ancestral homes
That the grandparents of my husband left behind
While young, when they had barely come of age.
The folks we met in offices and halls
Misunderstood, it seemed, how old we were,
That we were seeking information from
Not World War Two, but One. At last a clerk
Suggested going to the mountains where

Existing village churches might have saved
Recorded documents of births and deaths
From ravages of time and civil wars.
That day, I saw the note for services
At four o'clock, and so went back to slip
In through the chapel door, where worshipers
Were few, and old. More women there than men,
Who must have been at work, or timing out,
As was my husband, who would meet me soon.

For this service at mid-week, between seasons,
The space was much like chapels everywhere,
The wooden beams, maybe maple or oak,
With nave and pews, an elevated stage,
Communion table, golden tabernacle.
In the middle of an empty row, I sat
Apart, to show respect and deference
For form, the ritual and theater,
As if I knew what I was doing there.

The priest stepped back; the women led the chant.
Their voices droned in wild robust lament.
Although the syllables in Arabic were strange,
I still could sense the universal prayer
To Mary Mother of God, "*Salweh Marie.*"
The moody, thrumming sounds reached out to her
Who, having lost a son, could transform grief,
Today and at the hour of all our deaths,
Into a blessing, whole and tangible.

The resonating echo of their chant,
Its humming like cicadas in the fields
Where grass is cut and gathered into sheaves,
Is sung by those who live as if already dead,
To hover closer to pragmatic need
Then much of what we listen to at home,
The bouncy hymns against New England night,
To join the rituals of death to life
And savor loss before our loss of sight.

The Women in the Church

The women there had come, like me, alone,
To sing together in between the hours
Of morning shifts and dinner preparation,
In between provided roles of mother,
Daughter, grandmother, shedding one part,
Putting on another, second skin,
Student, speaker, leader, unemployed.
Gesticulations outside, dreams inside;
Identities at best, or else a mask.

One worshiper got up and joined me as
We stood to pray with all the others there.
She led me through responses with one arm
Linked through my arm, the other pointing to
The verse that said I'd be forgiven of
My trespasses if I'd forgive them theirs.
Her grip assured me she was merciful.
Her gaze through scrutinizing spectacles
Was not so sure. I lost my train of thought.

That she believed in me, though she could not
Have known how I had come or who I was,
Recalled uncertainty I'd kept at bay,
Walking, searching for a thing to do.
These women all engage themselves in tasks
That make them useful in the churchly things—
With flowers, cleaning, singing, ordering,
Withdrawing when official burghers come—
But I among them was a visitor,

A guest, not worthy to be there. I saw
A stronger mercy, shouldered in good will
That held these ancient offices in place,
These dovetailed beams, the passages of time.
At service end, I'll be released, outside,
To walk where hapless women can be stoned
Amid the noise of city crowds, the cars,
The taxis loitering, the screeching tires,
The horns and lights, the blinking on and off.

Unsigned Memorials to Mary

The unpaved path wound slowly down the hill
Until I passed the Virgin Mary's form,
Her hands extended from a plaster cape,
Or clamshell, ready to envelope any
Passerby who'd listen to her prayer.
Clichéd and real, she stood, nearly life-sized.
Below her on the ground, a chicken bustled
Near a cage, the little door ajar,
Its leg attached with tether loosely tied.

I took a photograph, and then I turned
To see the several people standing there
Assembled on the tiny cottage porch.
The older folk were not around, and by
The look of one young handsome boy, I saw
That I was caught up in a holy place
Of mourning. I put the camera down.
Not knowing what to do, I bowed, at least,
The way the Japanese bow from the waist.

Thinking back, I came to understand:
My path had cut right through their property.
The busy chicken that distracted me—
The way at home we have pets to distract
Us from the harshness of our busy lives—
Was not a pet, was being kept, not for
The present, nor the past, but the future,
The site undoubtedly memorial
To one who gave his life during the war.

Transported through the city in a cab,
I watched the buildings pass me in a blur,
Where statues of the Blessed Virgin stood
At lamp posts with flowers, tenderly arranged;
On traffic islands, Mary blue and white;
In a courtyard, Mary waiting open-armed.
Everywhere, in this part of the town,
Memorials to Mary floated on
The river of the city's dark renown.

Beirut Garden

We walked the city streets, arm in arm,
And talked of ways our common history
Unlocked the stories of our family,
The tribes and feudal lords, the olive farm;

Past windows, where the fragrances of thyme
And allspice, cumin, pepper, coriander
Spoke of celebrations with the grandeur
That flavors of the East and West combine;

Past the garden of the busy unmarked church
So far from home, and what we hoped to find
Among the many things we'd leave behind:
The answers to the questions of our search.

What will become of the Syrian refugees?
What will become of the Syrian refugees?

Notes

"The White Deer": *Nearly 200 white deer, a natural variant of the brown white-tailed deer, have been living on 7,000 acres of the former army depot in Romulus, New York, that will soon be put up for bid.*—Associated Press, *The Boston Globe*, November 16, 2015.

"Maps": An exercise in metonymy, after Emily Dickinson.

"Jumping Spider of My Mind": *The jumping spider, of Family Salticidae . . . For one thing, salticids do not necessarily follow a straight path in approaching prey. They may follow a circuitous course, sometimes even a course that takes the hunter through regions from which the prey is not visible.*—*Wikipedia*, accessed February 4, 2014.

"On Leaves": From a police report, Bridgewater, Massachusetts, *The Boston Globe*, December 1, 2020.

"III. Driving through Southern Lebanon": We have been to Lebanon many times; these poems are based on visits in 2008 and 2014 and reflections in between.

"Where No One Else Has Gone": Epigraph from *The Georgics of Virgil,* trans. from the Latin by David Ferry. New York: Farrar, Straus and Giroux, 2005 (115-117).

By sweet love urged
To roam Parnassus's lonely heights, it is
A delight to go where none has gone before,
No predecessor's wheel track to be seen
Upon the slope down toward the Castalian spring.

"Lamartine in Lebanon": From Alphonse de Lamartine, *A Pilgrimage to the Holy Land*, Vol II. New York: D. Appleton & Company, 1848 (333). *Autour de ces vieux témoins des âges écoulés, qui savent l'histoire de la terre mieux que l'histoire elle-meme.*

About the Author

Joyce Wilson is editor of *The Poetry Porch,* a literary magazine on the internet since 1997. Her poems appear in many journals, among them *The Hudson Review, The Lyric,* and *Think.* Her collections include *The Etymology of Spruce* (2010), *The Springhouse* (2010), *The Need for a Bridge* (2019), and *Take and Receive* (Kelsay Books, 2019). Her profiles of poets Eavan Boland, Julia Budenz, Etel Adnan, and Diana Der Hovanessian are on the Women Poets Timeline Project at *Mezzo Cammin.*

Taking classes as a special student at Harvard University for nearly a decade in the 1980s, Wilson received a B.A. through Harvard Extension and a M.Ed. from the Graduate School of Education. During that time, she studied writing poetry with Seamus Heaney and writing about poetry with Helen Vendler, in between seminars in English and American literature and education. She worked at Harvard's Woodberry Poetry Room as Assistant to the Curator and Managing Editor of *Harvard Review* (1991–1996) and taught English at Boston University (1987–1991, 1998–2002) and Suffolk University (2003–2013).

Wilson and her husband have lived in the same house in Scituate, Massachusetts, on the South Shore of Boston, since 1975. On their acre of land, they grow vegetables and flowers and raise flocks of chickens, who contribute their eggs and fertilizer to the ongoing process of growing things. They have traveled to Europe, the Middle East, and now Switzerland, to catch up with their daughter, married with two daughters, who is getting a doctorate in Art Criticism from the State University of New York at Stony Brook. She specializes in the art of the Middle East, the locale of her great-grandparents.

www.ingramcontent.com/pod-product-compliance
Lightning Source LLC
LaVergne TN
LVHW010542100826
845148LV00013B/2565

* 9 7 9 8 9 0 1 4 6 9 8 6 6 *